T0300700

LAO YANG

PEE POEMS

translated from Chinese by

JOSHUA EDWARDS
&
LYNN XU

LAO YANG

PEE POEMS

translated from Chinese by

JOSHUA EDWARDS

&

LYNN XU

ISBN 978-1-949918-03-8
First edition.

© by the author 2016.

English translation © 2022 Joshua Edwards and Lynn Xu.
All rights reserved.

No part of this publication may be reproduced or transmitted in any
form or by any means, electronic or mechanical, including photocopying,
recording, or any information storage or retrieval system, without
permission in writing from the publisher.

We would like to extend our deep appreciation to Yang, for his camaraderie
and for allowing us to translate *Pee Poems*. We would also like to thank
Elaine and Alex, for kindness and counsel; Samuel Amadon and Liz
Countryman, for publishing sections of this book in *Oversound*; Ken
Chen, Ha Jin, Rob Mazurek, Eileen Myles, and Zhang Er, for reading the
manuscript and offering ideas and endorsements; and Lynn's parents, who
helped a lot with the translation. Immense gratitude to our friends at the
Akademie Schloss Solitude, for introductions, support, and possibilities.
And lastly, infinite thanks to Dan Visel and Jennifer Kronovet of
Circumference Books, for their vision, insight, and stewardship.

Joshua Edwards and Lynn Xu

Published by:
Circumference Books
85 East End Avenue #14F
New York, New York 10028
www.circumferencebooks.com

Distributed by:
Small Press Distribution (SPD)
1341 Seventh Street
Berkeley, California 94710-1409
www.spdbooks.org

Printed by KOPA® *www.kopa.eu*

Contents

因為患有胃痙攣、腎焦慮和腦無力，我寫了幾首撒尿詩。

別叫我詩人，請叫我撒尿人——象含著一顆熱燙的"撒尿牛丸"那樣，在口中急急滾動，徐徐呼出：撒尿人

、。、，，

Suffering from stomach cramps, kidney problems, and muddled thinking, I wrote some pee poems.
Don't call me a poet, call me a piss person. Like a "juicy meatball," bursting suddenly in the mouth and spilling out: *piss person*

ˋ ○ ˋ. ˊ

第一部分：
撒尿詩
（36首）

PART ONE:
PISSING POEMS
36 VERSES

淚水化作尿液
澆灌出詩
#撒尿诗#

*

當自由哭泣的權利也被剝奪
尿失禁就成為所剩無多的自由之一

目睹了掌權者在人民的眼眶裡砌牆之後
我重新發明了撒尿

*

河床挽留了石頭／驅逐了河

*

鐘安靜下來／時間開始了⋯⋯

*

所有的淚水湧向海／海擠滿了鹽

Tears become urine
And irrigate the field of poetry
#Pee Poem#

*

When even the right to cry is denied
Incontinence is one of the few remaining liberties

Seeing rulers raise walls in the eyes of the people
I reinvent the act of pissing

*

The riverbed detains the stone / expels the river

*

The clock is silenced / time begins . . .

*

All tears flow to the sea / the sea fills with salt

7

岛

小陆　浮水

Island

Mainland, small land   floating

河流入耳

*

洪水翻洗了河床
塵埃抖落了喘息

*

每一個人都生活在自己親手而挖的陷阱裡

*

每一句真话
都能轻易地打折历史的一条腿

然而总有更多的人，以废话的语法
向历史插上一脚

*

宇宙是一鍋丸子湯／人根本談不上肉餡兒

A river enters an ear

*

The riverbed churns in the flood
Dirt gasps for air

*

Each person lives inside the hole they dig for themselves

*

A single spoken truth
Can easily hobble history

But always someone's fresh bullshit
Gives history a new leg to stand on

*

The universe is a pot of dumpling soup / humans are not
even worth mentioning as filling

人

*

人 从 众 / 众　从　人

*

天空是石頭海

海是石頭

*

萬物已就
被時間踩踏

等待寂靜降臨

Person

*

One of many / many of one

*

Sky a sea of stones

The sea is stone

*

All things have already
Been tread on by time

Waiting for stillness

詩

言寸土
言寺

Poetry

Shallow-dirt speak
Temple speak

這裡沒有答案
所以請別問題

*

故鄉不遠
一口就到

*

暗示的魔鬼　隱喻的小人

*

人即禽獸。
智者不爭

*

從來沒有理性地對待過垃圾
卻對製造垃圾充滿狂熱

16

Here there are no answers
So please ask no questions

*

Home isn't so distant
It's as close as your accent

*

The devil's suggestions   a petty person's doublespeak

*

People are animals too:
Profound thinkers don't disagree

*

We've never sensibly dealt with garbage
All our genius goes into its production

一种风景

秋风
木枯

清馆
客愁

A Kind of Landscape

Autumn wind
Weathered wood

Austere hall
Anxious guest

在這個時代
最需要被說出的話
是乾巴巴的真話

*

在時間調頭時、世界狹窄處，人當寂靜審思

*

在这个时髦的城市
乡巴佬又一次倒了大霉

*

流星泅渡了瀝青海
海鷗一小口一小口吞噬完自己

20

In this day and age
What needs to be spoken
Is the straight truth

*

When it's time for time's return, through the world's
narrow passage, one should contemplate quietly

*

The bumpkin meets misfortune once again
In this fashionable city

*

Meteors swim across an asphalt sea
The seagull consumes himself mouthful by mouthful

幽浮 UFO

来自另一个世界的风筝
载着另一个孤独的梦

UFO

A kite from another world arrives
Bearing another lonely dream

雾的眼睛
是风

*

我一路都在追随你的泪，
直到踏进那条奔流之河
……
最后搁浅在积盐之海。

*

转机出现在路上的时候
总会绊倒许多人

*

等凳瞪燈

*

你在自言自語

Fog's eyes
Are wind

*

I follow your tears all along,
Until I step into that rushing river
…
Finally adrift in the salty sea.

*

So many get squashed
In revolution's revolving door

*

Stay stool stare star

*

You are talking to yourself

文明史是一坨屎

*

嘲中有佛

*

整個世界都有待顛覆
以及對顛覆者和顛覆的顛覆

*

城市即暴政

The story of civilization is the tale of turd-mountain

*

Within ridicule dwells a buddha

*

The whole world awaits upending
And the upending of the upender's upending

*

City is tyranny

第二部分：
這個人
（43首）

PART TWO:
THIS PERSON
43 VERSES

我的人生硬梆梆

*

當我初踏人生途路 / 死神早已恭候多時

*

一個間歇性向內坍縮的洞穴 / 和一個努力自我娩出的胚胎

*

我站在玻璃後面看世界
世人在玻璃後面看我
我們相對無言
時間悄悄退走

*

少年你 / 處處處牆 / 執空心磚 / 開任意門

My life is a hard sort of hardness

*

When I took my first step on the path of life / the pale
rider had been a long time waiting

*

An intermittently collapsing cave / and an embryo
striving to deliver itself

*

From behind glass I observe the public
And the public sees me on display
We are all at a loss for words
And time tiptoes away

*

You in your youth / walled-in by walls / holding hollow
bricks / opening any door

帶刀少年在街頭奔跑
尋找真理姑娘

真理阻街賣春

少年以刀充嫖資
從此做了皮條客

*

自打在你的花瓣上初嘗你的鹽
我至今都在渴望水

*

在她的倆腿之間
夾著一道深淵
一座 海峽
一間肉室
一 壇城

A young man ran through the streets with a knife
Searching for true love, like in a song

Truth, impassible, turned tricks

The young man paid with a threat
And now he's a pimp

*

Alighting on your petals for the first time, tasting salt
I have until now always been longing for water

*

Between her two legs
An abyss
A strait
A meatroom
A mandala

雨敲打我的屋頂

我
望向遠方

*

道別之後
我獨自回家
身後悄悄跟著詩

Rain patters on my roof

I
Gaze into the distance

*

After saying goodbye
I return home alone
Following quietly behind me is the poem

鑰匙撑走了門
椅子卷起了路
暴雨沖走雨季
花朵摘下春天
我看著我
想著妳……

海啊湮沒了浪
魚兒背走了水
燈催眠了光
窗爬進了夜
我看著妳
忘了我……

The key now tears the door from its hinges
The chair now unpaves the road
A sudden rain washes away the rainy season
The flower plucks springtime
I look at myself
And think of you ...

O! sea that now vanishes in its waves
Fish that now carries away water
Lamp that now lullabies the light
Window that now crawls into night
I look at you
And now I forget myself ...

午夜列車情書

土豆把農夫丟向田野
石頭把洪荒拋入時間
星球把星團隱入星雲
眼珠被眼神牽進愛情
呵！
慈悲偉大的佛祖
長就慈悲為懷的佛陀
我親愛的人兒
妳看
我該怎樣向妳祖露心跡
失足洛水
步步蓮華

夜色如果溫柔
罪惡是否也願歇手
風景紛紛轉頭
鋼鐵展開歌喉

我靜止在動盪不安的旅途
心裏湧動溫柔

Midnight Train Love Letter

The potato flings farmer into field
The stone tosses the primordial into time
The planet hides galaxies in nebulae
Eyes are led by the gaze into love
O!
Great compassionate Buddha
Buddha who has long been compassionate
My dearest
Look at that
How can I show you my heart
Having lost my footing in the water
Step by lotus-flower step

If night is gentle
Evil will fall away
In succession the landscape turns
The singing voice that steel unfolds

This restless journey continues
And my heart is filled with tenderness

為著靈秀活潑的妳
也為恁多孤苦飄零的魂魄
為這罪惡昭彰的世界
也為你我得以在愛中避世

然而又不止溫柔
然而也心如止水
任憑眾生嗷嗷
塵世滔滔
我只靜靜安享此刻
心屬蓮花

For you, spirited and vivacious
And for the souls of the lonely multitude
For this world bright with evil
And for our love, I can turn away from it all

Except there's not simply gentleness
And yet there is a means to be at peace
With the suffering of sentient beings
And the discord of the mundane world
I experience this moment quietly
Heart like a lotus flower

致某久未回復的女詩人

硬著等你

To a Poet Who Hasn't Replied for a Long Time

Erect, waiting for you

和腫脹難消不眠的我
滾過紅塵

*

我要捅你的窟窿。
我要把你捅成一個窟窿。
我要在牆上捅窟窿。
我要把天捅出窟窿。
我要捅出天大的窟窿。

我多可笑。
最後，
我只在地上捅出了一個
我這麼大的窟窿。

And the swelling, sleepless me
Rolls around in red dust

*

I want to explore your openness.
I want to enter you until you're open.
I want to poke the wall until it opens.
I want to make in the sky an opening.
I want to make a sky-sized opening.

I'm so ridiculous.
In the end,
I only made a hole in the ground
That's the size of myself.

輕摁一次空格鍵
使自己消失
物在我無

牆與牆
人與人
字與字之間
是太空

*

一次次地從褪毛的開水中站起,張開失羽的肉膊,走著平衡木
如履尖刀,如履尖刀心懷狼毒狀如厲鬼,如履尖刀心自空明四
野寂然無聲,狼群呼哨奔突無止,奔突無止不暇喘息,不暇喘
息直達垂危無盡彌留,生生死死盡然可戀,是是非非與我何
干。一筐越冬的大白菜,過夏的鹹菜頭,故地重游,滾近前
坑,腳下無根頭上無纓,鹽漬的慘綠難解翻滾的鄉愁。

Lightly tap the space bar once
To disappear
To make way for things

Between walls
Between people
Between words
Is outer space

*

Emerging time and again from the boiling plucking-pot,
spreading out the body's featherless meat, balancing on
the board as on a sharp knife's blade, the sharp knife-like
heart demonic, the sharp knife-like heart silent as the
four quadrants of a field, silent but for the relentlessly
howling and loping wolves, breathlessly advancing,
breathlessly careening toward the end of life, pitiable life
and death, right and wrong having nothing to do with me.
In winter a basket of Chinese cabbage, pickled slaw in
summer, revisiting old haunts, rolling back into the
burrow, rootless underfoot and without a single strand up
top, even the greens' salty taste cannot stall the descent
into nostalgia.

一顆隕石
為火熱的人間灼傷

星空何其邈遠

*

孤獨者走向孤獨者
時間加密時間

虛妄者走向虛妄
空間解密空間

光牽引暗
力振盪弦

那麼
你是誰

A meteorite
Burns for the burning human world

The stars are set so deep in the sky

*

The lonely seek out the lonely
Time encrypts time

The vain search for the vain
Space decrypts space

Light gathers darkness
Power vibrates strings

So
Who are you

我本胡天胡地一胡人
象候鳥銜來了一顆異方的種子

*

一個全然的陌生人
走到哪裏都是異鄉

I'm a provincial barbarian
Like some migratory bird bringing a strange seed

*

To a complete stranger
Everywhere is a foreign country

馬爾法的頭一個早晨

雞叫三遍之後
汽車和火車都醒了

人還睡著

First Morning in West Texas

After three crows of the rooster
Cars wake up and the train as well

People still sleep

馬爾法的第二個早晨

火車從童年出走
不知去向
我背著故鄉
赤足追趕

三十年河西
三十年河東

在馬爾法
火車一再試圖喚醒我
可我的夢還沒做完
執意留在早晨

火車載著夢和故鄉遠去
早晨和我
留在馬爾法

Second Morning in West Texas

The train left my childhood
Not knowing its destination
Hometown at my back
I try to catch up, running barefoot

Thirty years west of the river
Thirty years east of the river

In Marfa
The train tries to wake me again and again
But my dreams, not yet over,
Are determined to last until morning

The train carries away dream and hometown
Morning and I
Remain in Marfa

我就是那焦慮的農夫
手裏攢著種子
赤著腳不停地走
到處尋找土地

他說

廢墟隆重且漫長
彷彿沒有邊際
文明及其葬禮
我不得不在瓦礫上播種

他說

招呼盲者來看
讓聾人聽
等啞巴講話

當暮色四合
我將失去他
你將失去我
我們將失去所有

I'm that anxious farmer
Seeds in hand
Ceaselessly walking barefoot
Searching all over for land

He says

The ruins are solemn and endless
Buddha is without limits
Civilization and its funerals
I have no choice but to sow seeds in rubble

He says

Greet the sightless to see
Let the deaf hear
Wait for the silent to speak

When twilight is nigh
I'm going to lose him
You're going to lose me
We're going to lose everything

我站在未來
回頭看見了末日
噩耗正陸續趕來
時間縮成一團

我看不見你
看不見我
往昔的太陽
無聲照耀

*

這些年我毀了所有好脾氣的人
我自己也毀了
被一種說不清楚的原因
像是不祥

像是某場約會
你等了一生
對方卻從未出發

I stand in the future
Looking back I see the last days
News of death arrives in waves
Time shrivels into a ball

I can't see you
Can't see me
The departed sun
Shines silently

*

Over the years I've destroyed good people
As I've destroyed myself
Without reason or explanation
It seems a bit unfortunate

It seems like that kind of rendezvous
For which you've waited a lifetime
To which the other never departed

我曾經寫過
"我一一撿起我的骨頭"

而現在
連狗都沒有了
我還撿它幹嘛

不祥有不祥的邏輯
狗有狗的邏輯
骨頭有骨頭的邏輯

約會沒有邏輯

我沒有邏輯

*

是的　我把自己活成了一綑荊棘
停止嘻笑　看看這世界
刺痛你是我最後的善意

I once wrote
"I pick up my bones one by one"

And now
I don't even have a dog
Why am I still picking up bones?

The unlucky have unlucky logic
Dogs have dog logic
Bones have bone logic

Rendezvous have no logic

I have no logic

*

Yes   I've cultivated my life into a bundle of thorns
Stop laughing   Look at the world
Thorn prick, you are my final kindness

夜半提燈
掘出深埋那我
仔細打量

*

日子實在是太好玩兒了
以致於沒有人想要去數它

她搖著橡皮筋兒
他捏著玻璃球兒
日子被她的橡皮筋一個一個地甩遠
又被他挨個兒捏小　再一個個的彈丟

在她們、他們都夠不著的地方
日子們正排著隊
等它們剩下的夥伴兒

等著的時候
誰也不說話

Late night lantern light
From the depths of darkness unbury me
For a closer look

*

These days are way too interesting
So interesting no one wants to count them anymore

She stretches a rubber band
He pinches a marble
One by one her rubber band ejects the days
And each is squeezed smaller by him then shot

To where neither of them can reach
The days are lining up
Waiting for their lingering companions

And while they wait
No one speaks

他在她掌心裡的海　拋錨已久
把那條船　改成了一座船屋

在船屋的陽台甲板上
他的笑容折射的陽光之下
她　曬日光浴

在陽光的蒸騰作用下
海　慢慢變成了　湖
湖　慢慢變成水窪
水窪　又變成了　雲
雲　又變成了　淚
淚　又變成水晶

水晶照見了一切：

在他的一根木棍裡
藏著整個海的水

而她的一塊手帕裡
則裹著海的所有鹽

He has long been anchored   in the sea of her palm
Having converted that boat   into a houseboat

On the deck of the houseboat
His smile refracts the sun
She   bathes in its light

Under the sun, with transpiration
Sea   slowly becomes   lake
Lake   slowly becomes   puddle
Puddle   becomes   cloud
Cloud   becomes   tears
Tears   become   crystal

Crystal illuminates everything:

A single one of his sticks
Contains all the ocean's water

And wrapped in one of her handkerchiefs
Is the entirety of the sea's salt

船屋下的木板
重新又長出了樹的腳

＊

我从小
就被摁倒在红旗下
摁倒在他人的荣光里

直到现在　我还会
因为提不上一条完整的裤子
而兀自羞耻

＊

每个人都有一部历史。
我象狗一样孤独地看守着自己的历史
记忆是那条栓着我的链子

＊

一花若是一世界，一口痰、一泡屎當作如是觀。
你愛拈花微笑、我自捧屎不語。

The boards of the houseboat's hull
Resprout the tree's feet

*

Ever since I was little
I've been pressed down by this red flag
Pressed under its magnificent light

Even now   I still
Because I don't have a decent pair of pants
Feel shame

*

Everyone has a history.
With dog-like solitude I guard my own
Memory is the chain that holds me back

*

If the world is in a blossom, then it's in spit and shit too.
You love to pick flowers, I silently suppress a turd.

仿宋体自传

潘在树林里飞快地逃窜。
这本是他的领地，如今却象被捅了一棍的马蜂窝。

3781，3782，……3787……
普罗米修斯数着那头残鹰用鏽铁般的喙啄向他那颗暗红色的肝
脏，一股生鲜的肉腥味在他身周弥散

Imitation of Autobiography

Pan flees through the woods.
Once his usual haunt, this place is now like a poked hornet's nest.

3781, 3782,......3787......
Prometheus counted the times the cruel eagle's rusty beak pecked
at his crimson liver, the smell of fresh flesh enshrouding him

握著這顆靈魂石頭一樣硬
砸一塊玻璃？
或者上帝的腦門

*

人看我寫詩
我看詩寫我
詩
不看

*

眼睛裡的海 / 海中的雲 / 雲外的天空 / 空的心

Holding this stone-like soul:
Should I smash a pane of glass?
Or God's forehead

*

People watch me write poems
I watch poems write me
Poems
Don't see

*

Sea inside the eye / clouds inside the sea / sky outside the
clouds / an empty heart

月亮之下
甚麼秘密也藏不住

一輪清光
照徹洪荒

*

在夜晚
每個人升起各自的星空
邂逅一再復生的自己
遭遇橫無際涯的黑暗

*

石頭看我一眼

Beneath the bright moon
No secret can be hidden

A circle of clear light
Breaks on an ancient land

*

At night
Each person is lifted into their own starry sky
To meet a self who has been resurrected again and again
To encounter the boundlessness of darkness

*

The rock casts a glance my way

起步索天問，歇馬眠何鄉？
長風拂廣野，碧綠轉青黃。
大荒窮人跡，隻影間地天。
曾結無情遊，空心照雲漢。

*

褪去所有堅硬的外殼之後
我發現人類之美
所有的言說止於瞬間的凝視
於永動之中
於永動之中

At the outset questioning heaven, where to rest one's
    horse?
Trade winds blow across the plains, transforming deep
    green into greens and yellows.
Wasteland bereft even of the poor, lonely as a cloud
    between the earth and sky.
Relentlessly they travel together, hearts empty as the
    dark zodiac.

                                *

After removing the hard outer shell
I discover the beauty of humans
All words arrested by a glimpse
In perpetual motion!
In perpetual motion!

第三部分：
這國
（46首）

PART THREE:
THIS COUNTRY
46 VERSES

一寸河山一寸病

*

扒開昏寐的眼睛植入鐵一樣黑涼的現實⋯⋯

*

一個遺臭萬年的時代
人民吃屎都能吃出花樣兒的時代

一個活死人的時代

*

今天這國 / 國歌是地道的噪音 / 噪音是正統的國歌

*

知識份子的中式鄉愁看不到盡頭 ⋯⋯

A measure of territory, a degree of illness

*

Pry open sleepy eyes and plunge into the cool, hard night of reality

*

The infamy of this era will endure
It's an era of prodigious and imaginative shit-eating

It's a time for the living dead

*

Today in this nation / the national anthem is just noise / noise is the original national anthem

*

Intellectuals have limitless nostalgia for China

牆比人走得凶

*

濁世不宜飲清酒

*

在暗夜掌權的土地上
每一個人都失眠

*

眾人將黑暗認作子宮
你將黑暗烤製成黑紙

*

狼來了又來
直到羊群筋疲力盡

Walls advance more fiercely than folk

*

It's improper to drink clear spirits in a muddled world

*

Wherever darkness controls the land
Everyone suffers from insomnia

*

They regard darkness as a womb
You bake darkness into black paper

*

Wolves come and come again
Until the sheep are utterly exhausted

主關起籠門清點人數
發現唯獨少了撒旦

但主一轉身
籠中人就看見了他們高貴的死神

*

曠野裡一齊抬起了悲哀的龜頭

*

孩子們走向灰塵
灰塵走向輪子和履帶
輪子和履帶走進陰沈的門
陰沈的門
關起了黑暗

God locks the cage, takes an inventory of people
And finds only Satan missing

When God turns his back
The caged glimpse their elegant Lord of the Flies

*

Simultaneously lifting sorrowful penises in the wild

*

Children walk toward dust
Dust moves in the direction of dozers
Dozers enter the gloomy door
The gloomy door
Encloses the darkness

大地上長著草
草上長著露珠
露珠上長著太陽
太陽上長著黑洞

黑洞很黑
黑下了這一切

*

流星泅渡了瀝青海
海鷗一小口一小口吞嚥完自己

*

屎是臭的
從來都是
沒被拉出來的屎不臭
除非有人把它從肛腸科里扒出來

Grass grows on earth
The dew gathers on grass
On the dewdrop the sun gleams
In the sun the black hole grows

Black holes are very black
They black out all of this

*

Meteors swim across the asphalt sea
And mouthful by mouthful the seagull swallows itself

*

Turds smell
It's always been so
But before shit is shat it doesn't
Unless someone pulls proctologically

最初我們都是荒地

後來長出了什麼
都是精心算計過的

         *

土地抱緊農夫
車輪載來城市

墓地在城鄉之間連片生長
文明史

         *

鳥兒的晨鳴從黎明傳來 / 抵達黑暗時 / 成為嘹亮的號角

At first we are all just barren land

What grows from this?
Everything is meticulously planned

*

The land embraces the farmer
And the wheel conveys the city

Cemeteries sprawl from city to country
A history of civilization

*

Birdsong arrives with daybreak / and reaching darkness /
becomes a loud horn

往奶粉裡摻腎結石
往疫苗裡摻後遺症
往房地產裡摻人肉
往包子裡摻政治
往漢字裡摻刀具
往奢侈品裡摻共產主義
往災區摻黨和國家領導人
往西方發達國家摻子孫後代
往監獄摻良心犯
往星空裡摻溫家寶
往眼淚裡摻水泥
往腦子裡摻屎

Into baby formula add kidney stones
Into the vaccine mix side effects
Into real estate put human flesh
Into steamed buns stuff politics
Into the Chinese language stick knives
Into luxury goods incorporate Communism
Into the disaster area introduce Party and State leaders
Into the developed nations of the West mingle
    descendants of future generations
Into the prisons stuff prisoners of conscience
Into the starry sky put Wen Jiabao
Into your tears mix cement
Into your head add shit

天問——致可能的同路人

如何在糞坑裡吃飯
如何在荊棘上睡覺
如何在血泊裏洗澡
如何在炮烙上納涼
如何在凌遲中談情
如何在冰窟裏取暖
如何在毒氣室呼吸
如何在集中營做愛
如何在刀尖上舞蹈
如何在割喉後歌唱
如何在廢墟上安居
如何在彈雨中辯論
如何在礦井下遙看地平線
如何在黑鐵屋裏仰望星空
如何在地獄耕作
如何在天堂施捨

如何把如何拋給別人
如何用回答砸倒自己

Spiritual Questions for Fellow Travelers

How to eat in a cesspit
How to sleep on thorns
How to bathe in a bloodbath
How to enjoy a cool breeze on a pillar of fire
How to romance during a slow death
How to gather heat inside an ice cave
How to breathe the anguish of poison air
How to screw in a concentration camp
How to dance on the tip of a knife
How to sing with a slit throat
How to make a home of the ruins
How to debate under a hail of bullets
How to see the horizon in a mineshaft
How to gaze at the stars in a pitch-black room
How to farm in hell
How to give alms in heaven

How to pawn *how* off on others
How to smash yourself in response

漢語的內戰

优雅羞辱優雅
体面姦污體面
智慧調戲智慧
信任煽動信任

友谊圍毆友誼
亲情霸凌親情
爱情買賣愛情
忠诚掌摑忠誠

建筑拆毀建築
法律玩弄法律
公平吊打公平
正义追殺正義

经济賄賂經濟
文化輪姦文化
政治傾軋政治
社会凌遲社會

Civil War of the Chinese Language

Elegance humiliates *élégance*
Dignity defiles decorum
Wisdom harasses wisdom
Trust incites trust

Friendship gangs up on friendliness
Affection bullies fondness
Love buys and sells love
Devotion slaps fealty

Building demolishes construction
The law toys with the law
Fairness clobbers fairness
Justice hunts down righteousness

Economics bribes political economy
Culture gang rapes culture
Politics overturns politics
Community tortures society to death

凡應升舉的均得昇舉
凡需踩抑的逐一踩抑
但能姑且的一概姑且
但能殃及的盡數殃及

*

在痛苦的海洋上
人們各懷鬼胎
忙著繁殖歡樂

在歡樂的針尖上
朗日空照
無人問津

Whatever should rise will be lifted up
What should be crushed will be squashed
Yet all that's contingent will remain conditional
And whatever should be ruined will be ravaged

*

In the ocean of pain
Lurk the dark designs of those
Who propagate happiness

On joy's sharp blade
Gleams the sun's empty light
No one could care less

為甚麼悲傷如此短暫
歡愉卻如此漫長

路上人們的臉上都洋溢著輕快的歡愉
像垃圾車一路揚起的灰塵

*

：媽媽，我的世界裏有地獄！
：那有天堂嗎？
：得自己蓋。

Why is sadness so short
And delight so long

Faces of people on the road are brimming with joy
Like the dust stirred up by a garbage truck

*

—Mother, my world has hell inside it!
—Is there also heaven?
—You have to build it yourself.

一片雲變幻莫測
成為了另一片雲
一刀肉千刀萬剮
塞進了另一刀肉
一陣哆嗦
源自另一陣哆嗦
一場雨
追上了另一場雨

*

把鬼屋還給鬼
把垃圾場還給垃圾
把夢還給枕頭

把種子
還給它媽的植物

A cloud changes unpredictably
Becoming another cloud
A cut of flesh made mincemeat
Is stuffed into another cut
Sudden shivering
Issues forth from another shiver
One downpour
Catches up to another downpour

*

Give the haunted house back to the ghost
Return the garbage dump to the garbage
Restore the dream to the pillow

Put the seeds
Back in the goddamn plant

敕勒川，
蒼山下。
好一座壇城、
和风吹作漫天沙。
一條散漫的河
在堅硬如牆的大地上流淌
荒誕不經地把自己舉向廢墟
把廢墟舉向星空
把星空舉向虛無

*

在火車呼嘯的村莊
孩子們開始赤足奔跑

三十年後
當他垂危返鄉
車窗外
整個田野都在燃燒
發出比火車還要尖厲的呼嘯

100

High plains of the High Cart Tribes,
Below Cang Mountain.
What a mandala,
With a gentle breeze that fills the sky with sand.
A lazy and undisciplined river
Flows along the earth like a wall
Paradoxically running upward toward the ruins
Raising the ruins toward the stars
Lifting the stars into the void

*

In the village where the train roars
Children set off running barefoot

Dying he returns to his hometown
Thirty years later
Outside the car window
Entire fields are in flames
Their shrieks are more piercing than the train's

在片片黑幕的後面隱身著上帝

神亮起電子光哺飼它饑餓的子民
牧者的羊群高舉虔誠的玻璃
遵照神的意旨
刷屏或是視禱
將主的福音折播向浩渺無垠的深空

人機的歡愉廣布宇宙

*

狼們都披好了羊皮
羊們也都磨尖了牙齒

沉睡者摟緊夢遊者
時間醒了

Behind the subtlety of dark scenery is divinity

God powers electricity to feed his hungry people
The shepherd's flock lifts the pious glass
According to divine will
Create fresh content or pray
Broadcast the gospel into the vastness of space

The joy of man and machine permeates the universe

*

The wolves are all dressed in sheep's clothing
The sheep have sharpened their teeth too

The sleeper embraces the sleepwalker
Time wakes up

時間醒了
像億萬顆輝煌的太陽
閃爍在碎世界的碎玻璃堆上

*

——不
太陽早就死了
死在永恆延燒的灰燼裏

受了人造光的引誘
時間在碎玻璃鋒利的邊沿爬動
拼湊不成人形

Time wakes up
Like billions of brilliant suns
Glittering on the broken shards of the broken world

*

—No
The sun died long ago
Dead in the eternally-burning ashes

Seduced by artificial light
Time crawls along the sharp edges of broken glass
Unable to conjure the human form

面對坦克和鏈車
唯一不能被摧毀的
就是廢墟

站在街頭
我總是背靠廢墟
廢墟靠磚頭保護自己
我要手撫磚頭才能站立

*

曠野裡
龜頭的淪亡
乳頭的受難
木頭和行頭一起漂浮
磚頭和人頭一起風化
榔頭和骨頭一起破碎
豬頭和龍頭一起懸掛

石頭和骷髏頭一起對話

Up against tanks and bulldozers
The only things that cannot be destroyed
Are ruins

Standing on the street
I always lean on the ruins
The ruins protect themselves with bricks
I need the bricks to help me stand

*

In the wilderness
The penis perishes
The nipple suffers
Wood floats with fashionable outfits
Brick erodes alongside human heads
Hammers break with bones
Pig heads hang with faucets

Rocks talk to skulls

這首詩需要大聲地、用力地唱出：

藍藍的天上白雲飄，
白雲下面你在跑——
因為前邊有泡屎～～
去晚了吃不著……

This verse needs to be loudly, vigorously sung:

Above the blue sky are white clouds,
And below the white clouds you run—
Because a pile of shit's up ahead
And if you get there late you get none...

八月——2008年8月9日北京

狗屎在马厩里发酵
热气俯仰鼻息
暴风雨旅途劳顿
趴在门外喘息

党仍在勃起
人民依然亢奋

无聊和疲倦
比睡眠来得更硬
但他们确已睡着
在彼此玲珑的微巢

马驰过旷野

August 9, 2008, Beijing

Dog crap ferments in the stables
Hot fumes waft up to a nose
A storm fatigued from its journey
Lies panting at a door that is closed

The Party still has an erection
The people still stand at attention

Disinterest and exhaustion
Arrives more insistent than sleep
But they are already sleeping
Each in the fine nest of another

Horses gallop across a vast range

最終，植物吃光了所有的肉

植物尖叫著奔向沉默
沉默轉身就走
走踉踉蹌蹌
踉蹌長途跋涉
跋涉口乾舌燥
燥清心寡慾
慾磕磕絆絆
磕絆一路瘋長

最終，植物吃光了所有的肉

Finally the plants eat all the meat

The plants rush shrieking toward silence
Silence turns to leave
Stumbumbling
Staggering on a long and difficult trek
Trudging with dry mouth and tongue
Parched and austere
Desiring to tripitytrip
To tumble the whole weird way

Finally the plants eat all the meat

一旦上路
路就再也看不到盡頭

死也不是終點
而只不過是一枚倉促、
倔強的人形路標

路在大地上顛簸伸展
猶如牧童手裏散漫的鞭子
抽打著草木、虛空
以及虛空中飄蕩著的灵魂

勢必是踉蹌的
即便不受阻于腳下呲牙般的巉石
也難免失足於靈魂的坑窪

路拉扯著腳
腳拍打著路
漸行漸遠
漸漸不見

Once on the road
The end of the road cannot be seen

Nor is death an end
It's just a sudden road sign
In human shape

The road waves and winds across the earth
Like an unruly whip in a young shepherd's hand
Lashing the grass and the void
And the soul that lingers in the void

Stumbling is inevitable
Even if the chasm doesn't get ahold of you
It's hard to avoid losing your footing in the pit of the soul

The road drags the foot
The foot smacks the road
They drift apart
And gradually fade

在地下：蛇鼠

我擺脫街上的貓
喘著氣回到洞口
忘了扭亮電燈
我摸著黑走向深處的床

我摸著黑走著，突然
它咬住了我的嘴！
它咬住了我的嘴！
它咬住了我的嘴！

我忍著疼掙扎著後退
我忍著疼感到後悔
就在光亮出現的一刹那
我笑了
我看見它吐出了我的骨頭　陰險地走掉

我一一撿回我自己

Underground Snake Rat

I escape from a cat in the street
I return out of breath to the mouth of the cave
I completely forget to turn on the light
I grope in the dark toward a bed in the depths

I grope in the dark going forth, then suddenly
It bites me on the mouth!
I'm bitten on my mouth!
It has bitten me on the mouth!

I stagger back in pain
Full of hurt and regret
I laugh just as a light turns on
I laugh
Seeing my bones spit out   I sneak out

And pick myself up piece by piece

因為跌倒在廢話裡
神仙也就下了凡
坐在立交橋下的馬路牙子上
擼肉串兒喝啤酒

油煙飄去處
新栽的草木蔫頭搭腦
一半已死一半殘喘

吳帶當風濕衣衫

三十年的塵埃吃下
整個城鄉結合部
顛簸在廢話的路上

幸運的是
所有的噩耗都還在路上

所有的人形容器都已經滿溢

Because I descend into nonsense
The gods fall to the impermanent earth
And sit by the street under the overpass
Eating kebabs and drinking beer

Where the exhaust drifts
The freshly-planted plants wither and droop
Half-dead and half-gasping

Wu paints robes like wind, wet clothes

Having eaten dust for thirty years
The city and countryside coalesce
And romp together down absurdity's road

Fortunately
The real bad news is yet to come

All the personified vessels will spill over

大地炙烤著鹽、痛苦和血跡
經年的雨水卻懸而未決
不知道該往哪兒落

迷走的人
撞響聳起的夢
飄散的魂兒帶著小板凳兒
尋故鄉

鐵了的心吃了秤砣
折了的翅兒做了網兜
秤砣愛蹦床
網兜撈不著

再大的雨
也不能證明天漏了

何況
雨一直沒下
燒烤遍天下

Earth is scorched to reveal salt, pain, and bloodstains
Years of rainwater hang in the balance
Not knowing where to fall

A person, lost and adrift
In the shadow, a towering dream
A wandering soul with a wooden stool
Searches for home

An iron heart devours a weight
A bent wing becomes a net
The weight loves a trampoline
And can't be caught in a net

No amount of rain
Can prove the sky is leaking

Besides
It hasn't rained
And all the world is barbeque

要怎樣才能回到鄉下
鄉下的鄉，鄉下的下？
無非是胸口碎大石
赤腳蹈釘板

大救星，
把田野連根拔起
升起天堂

許我等小民

坐在場院看電視

……
……
……

拉扯不清的田壟上
小民被連根拔起
倒栽進水裡

How does one get back to the countryside
Way out in country, way way outside?
Just a cracked stone in the chest
And barefoot on a bed of nails

Chairman:
Uproot the fields
And rise to the heavens

Allow me and other nobodies
To sit in the yard and watch TV

......
......
......

On the impure path raised between fields
Folks are pulled up by the roots
And then thrust headfirst into water

水裡升起天堂
天堂裡座著救星
仰望星空數星星

……
……
……

鄉下的下，鄉下的鄉
要怎樣才能回到？
也無非就是
胸口蹈釘板
赤腳碎大石

Paradise rises from the water
In heaven sits the savior
Gazing skyward and counting stars

. . . . . .
. . . . . .
. . . . . .

Way, way outside, way out in the country,
How do you find your way back?
It's nothing more than
A chest dancing against a bed of nails
And bare feet shattering stone

東方不敗

攬鏡自已
海西客菊花一緊
長安丸泊進曼哈頓

　（燈火照大荒，

吞噍自己
膝下獨子瘸行
口吐（tù）蓮花

……何期邈雲漢）

抱緊自己
歷史的穿牆術
解近渴

　（拈花　相逢　一笑）

Invincible East

Get a load of yourself
Chrysanthemum-clenched guest from the western sea
The famous ship reaches Manhattan

   (Lights shine on a vast absurdity,

Consume yourself
Only child, lame and limping
Spitting out—*ptooey*—lotus

... In the age of imperial beauty)

Embrace yourself
History's implacable advance
Slakes this immediate thirst

   (Flower mudra   meeting   in laughter)

Translators' Note

Joshua Edwards & Lynn Xu

In the fall of 2016, Lao Yang traveled to the States from China and spent a few months in our home in West Texas while we were away for work. It was there that he finished *Pee Poems*. The train that tries to wake him again and again in these pages is the same train that succeeds in waking us each morning, and perhaps this serves as a metaphor for the biggest challenge we faced as translators of this book: how to bring forth the wonderful spirit of its author, who chooses the difficult dream over an easy life.

We became friends with Yang in 2012, when we all lived at Akademie Schloss Solitude, an artist residency in Germany. He was there as a music/sound fellow, but beyond his performances and various other creative practices, he is known as a gardener, builder, teacher, and promoter of experimental music. For many years Lao Yang ran an art space and music store in the 798 district in Beijing, and in fact we first crossed paths with him there, very briefly, in 2009. By that time, financial and political forces had pushed out nearly all the other artist-run spaces, so his tiny store, with a wall of floor-to-ceiling CDs, was particularly memorable. We both recollect him calling out a greeting from the loft above. Within a year, authorities would ransack this space and violently force him out.

In an interview conducted during the protest he staged immediately after the destruction of his store and home, Lao Yang stated: "This is not performance art. Art is like a lame act of charity in the face of life's cruelty. When someone sets himself ablaze with gasoline, just to illuminate his sabotaged home, it naturally eclipses the impact of any work of art.... Until we have secured our rights, we cannot practice art, cannot live with art, cannot think artistically or observe this world with an artistic eye." Years later he explained his own creative practice to us in this context, saying that it is not art, but what comes before, when art is not possible. "Don't call me a poet, call me a piss person," he writes at the beginning of this collection.

Yang has also called himself a "noise maker and its noise." From his writing it is clear that the clamor he makes is directed beyond the ear, to the social and spiritual origins of the listener's attention. One of our easier tasks was conveying the urgency of *Pee Poems*, but what proved much more difficult was rendering the mix of subtlety and straightforwardness in his language. In his Chinese text, there is often an orthographic interrogation of characters. Take for example the aphoristic fragment "人 从 众 / 众 从 人" (literally: "person from multitude / multitude from person"), which simply shows us the movement from the pictograph for "person" (人) to the compound ideographs "from" (从) and "multitude" (众). This is a particularly beautiful palindrome in which the movement from person to multitude is mirrored, to show both creation and decreation; or, there is a contract in the language itself (the formation of the characters) between the singular and the plural, which the author is helping us remember. The multitude is built from the person, and that conjunction itself—from—requires a movement from one (person) to two. Our thoughts went first to the seventh section of George Oppen's "Of Being Numerous" ("Obsessed, bewildered // By the shipwreck / Of the singular // We have chosen the meaning / Of being numerous."), but this and other references would be politically misleading, so in the end we decided to make the simplest translation we could think of: "One of many / many of one."

Another kind of challenge is exemplified by the poem "Civil War of the Chinese Language," in which Yang deftly and playfully broaches historical and political tensions by pitting the Chinese language against itself, setting traditional characters (used in Hong Kong, Taiwan, and a few other places) against simplified characters (the official script of Mainland China). In English, we juxtaposed some words with Germanic roots with their counterparts of French origin to convey a sense of how historical conflict becomes embedded in language, but we also just followed Yang's lead and fooled around with words.

Language play and puns are frequently used in *Pee Poems*, and readers of our English translation might think of this book in conversation with works by Marcel Duchamp and John Cage. Seeing as Lao Yang was one of the early apostles of sound art and experimental music in China in the 2000s, these readers would not be wrong—one can imagine him nodding in agreement to Cage's

"Farting, don't think, just fart," or Duchamp's "Art is not about itself but the attention we bring to it." Or one might think of the Black Mountain poets or the anti-poems of Nicanor Parra. But focusing on Western aesthetics obscures this young Chinese poet's radicality, as well as his place in traditions that go back many hundreds of years. In the style of some Tang Dynasty poets, Lao Yang writes intensely about solitude, longing, and friendship, but like Zhuangzi, he is concerned primarily with the most complex and elusive of concepts: freedom and peace. Having a creative practice that actively promotes these ideas and denounces their antagonists, Yang lives with risks that most of us can't imagine.

Tied closely to these themes of freedom and attention is Lao Yang's spiritual inquiry, which recalls Chan and Zen thinkers like Shiwu, Hanshan, Dōgen, and Ryōkan. The association is made explicit in Yang's short piece "Poetry," in which he takes apart the title character, *shi* (詩). The constituent parts, or radicals, are thus made to speak for themselves: "言寸土 / 言 寺" ("Shallow-dirt speak / Temple speak"). As Red Pine points out in the preface to his wonderful translation of *Poems of the Masters*, the second part (寺) of the word for poetry (詩) was originally written *zhì* (志), "meaning 'from the heart,' and the later form was simply the result of calligraphic shorthand and subsequent convention. Hence the word for poetry does not mean 'language of the court/temple' but the 'language of the heart'."

In working together to translate this book by our friend, we were constantly reminded of Yang's great kindness, humor, and intelligence. We thought back on conversations about philosophy, plants, food, travel, love, and so much more, and we reminisced about his unique combination of fierceness and grace. Over the years, Lao Yang's bravery and integrity have inspired us to examine our own beliefs and choices, so it's been a distinct pleasure to discuss and think about his writing. In a speech translated by Rosmarie Waldrop, Paul Celan said that "a poem, being an instance of language, hence essentially dialogue, may be a letter in a bottle thrown out to sea with the—surely not always strong—hope that it may somehow wash up somewhere, perhaps on a shoreline of the heart." The act of translation may be an answer to and an echo of that hope, and we thank you for reading our version of Lao Yang's *Pee Poems*.

Biographies

Lao Yang

Lao Yang was born in northeastern China. He founded one of China's first independent advocacy spaces dedicated to experimental music and sound art in Beijing. A recipient of a Jean-Jacques-Rousseau fellowship, he was a resident at the Akademie Schloss Solitude, and he has performed at venues and festivals around the world.

Joshua Edwards

Joshua Edwards was born on Galveston Island. He's the author of several books, including *The Double Lamp of Solitude* (Rising Tide Projects, 2022), *Architecture for Travelers* (Editions Solitude, 2014), and *Imperial Nostalgias* (Ugly Duckling Presse, 2013), and he translated María Baranda's *Ficticia* (Shearsman Books, 2010). He coedits Canarium Books.

Lynn Xu

Lynn Xu was born in Shanghai. She's the author of two full-length collections, *And Those Ashen Heaps That Cantilevered Vase of Moonlight* (Wave Books, 2022) and *Debts & Lessons* (Omnidawn, 2013), as well as two chapbooks, *June* (Corollary Press, 2006) and *Tournesol* (Compline, 2021). She coedits Canarium Books and teaches at Columbia University.

CIRCUMFERENCE BOOKS

Circumference Books is a press for poetry in translation.
Our books highlight the process of translation and how that work is
rooted in collaboration. Each multi-lingual project foregrounds original
design solutions, making visual the relationships between languages,
cultures, writers, and translators. Circumference Books supports the creative
and urgent work of bridging cultures and languages. Our projects spotlight
non-national languages and foster cross-linguistic poetic exchange.

Circumference Books would not be possible without our

MEMBERS

Carrie Olivia Adams · Elina Alter · Samuel Amadon
Stephanie Anderson · Sally Ball · Mary Jo Bang
Jessica Baran · Alexandra O. Betlyon · Paul Bisagni
Patrick Brosnan & Christine Brosnan · Jennifer Chang
Don Mee Choi · Hillary Cookler · Mónica de la Torre
Sharon Dolin · Danielle Dutton · Elaine Garza
Gabrielle Giattino · Michelle Gil-Montero · Eric Giroux
Sonja Greckol · Sandra Guerreiro · Stefania Heim & Peter Pihos
Rita Kronovet · Steven Kronovet · Brett Fletcher Lauer · Angie Lee
Martha Lewin & Jack Egan · E.J. McAdams · Tamerra Moeller
Trey Moody · Erín Moure · Collier Nogues · Idra Novey
Carl Phillips · Josephine Pickford Beeman · James Shea & Dorothy Tse
David Shook · Stephen Sparks · Terence Stevick
Christina Svendsen · Tree Swenson · Zach Tackett · Hugh Thomas
Lawrence Venuti · Michael Welt · Jesse Wilbur
Jeffrey Yang · Matvei Yankelevich

Find out more about membership:

www.circumferencebooks.com